Get set! Go!

Story by Shigeo Watanabe   Pictures by Yasuo Ohtomo

3B

OVERCOMING
OBSTACLES

PHILOMEL BOOKS

Text © Shigeo Watanabe .1980 • Illustrations © Yasuo Ohtomo 1980 • American text © Philomel Books 1981 • All rights reserved
First United States of America publication 1981, Philomel Books,
a division of The Putnam Publishing Group, 200 Madison Avenue, New York, N.Y. 10016
Printed in the United States • Library of Congress CIP information at back of book.

Here we go!

It's an obstacle race.

First, along the beam quickly...

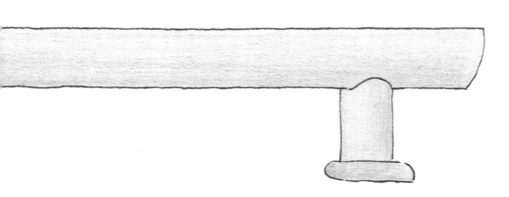

7

Ow!

Next, around the bar…

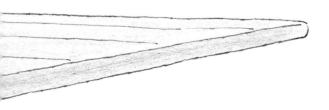

Thump!

Over the horse...

15

Oh, dear!

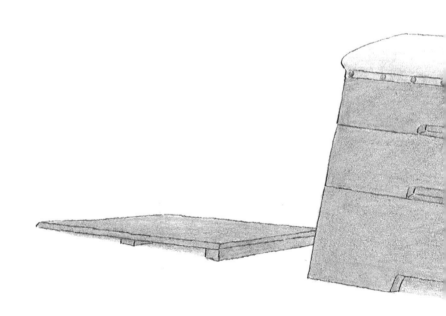

Through the tunnel ...

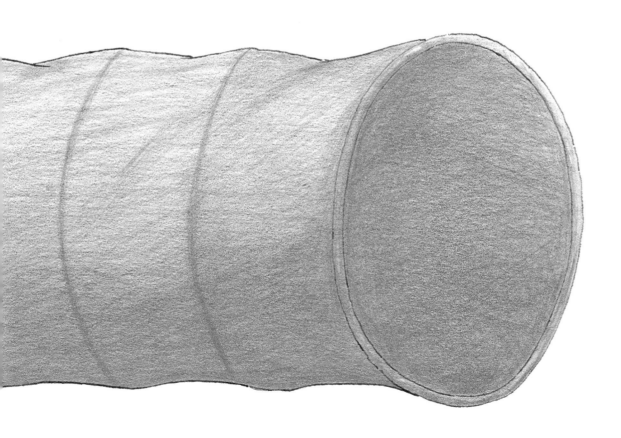

Oops!

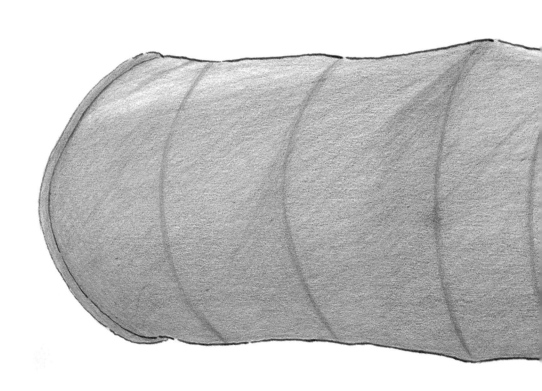

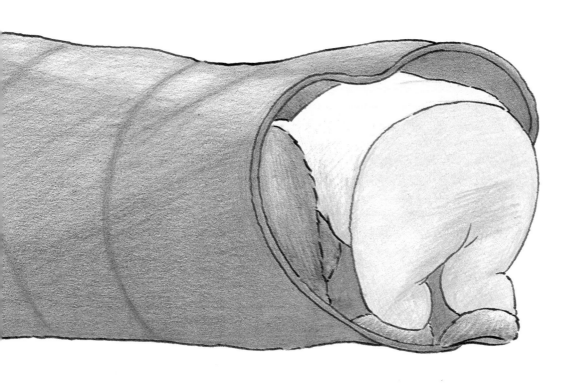

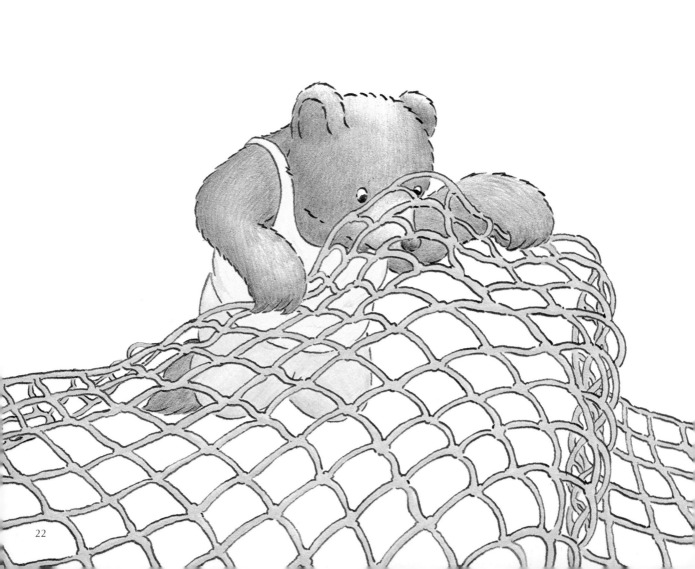

Under the net…

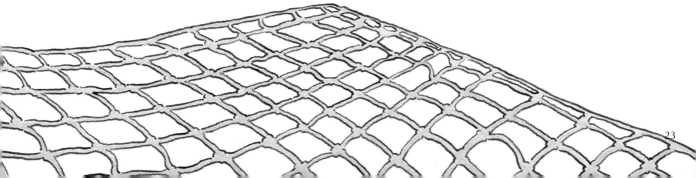

Oh, no!

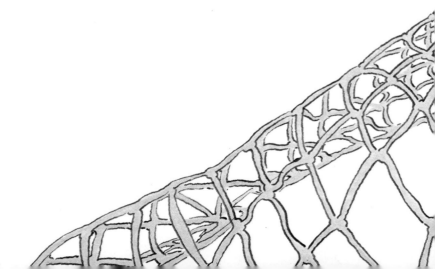

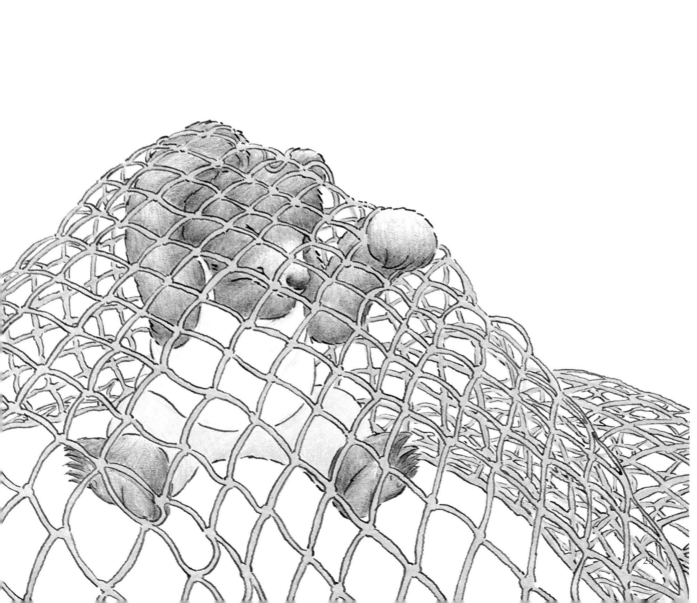

I'm nearly there…

Over the finish line! Hurrah!
Did I win?

Library of Congress Cataloging in Publication Data
Watanabe, Shigeo, 1928–
Get set! Go!
(An I can do it all by myself book; 3)
SUMMARY: Though Bear does not win the
obstacle race, he demonstrates perseverance in
getting through it.
[1. Obstacle racing—Fiction. 2. Bears—Fiction]
I. Ohtomo, Yasuo. II. Title.
PZ7.W2615Ge 1981 [E] 80-22373
ISBN 0-399-20780-5
ISBN 0-399-61175-4 (lib. bdg.)

Typography by Antler & Baldwin.
Set in Optima Medium.
Composition by Frost Brothers, Inc.
Printed by Federated Lithographers-Printers, Inc.
Bound by Economy Bookbinding Corp.